THIS BOOK
BELONGS TO:

Henry Hump
Born to Fly

Written by
Steve Tiller

Illustrated by
Robert Cremeans

MichaelsMind.
ATLANTA

To Anna and Olivia –
Stay Proud
Touch the Sky!

Steve Tiller

Steve Tiller, Author
Robert Cremeans, Illustrator / Creative Director
Kathryn L. Tecosky, Editor

Special thanks to: Our Families, CCAD , The Chicago Bromleys, David & Melissa Abbey, Brian Bias our Apple guru,
and lots of hugs to Mary Huggins, grammarian extraordinarie!

Library of Congress Cataloging-in-Publication Data
Tiller, Steve

Summary: It is a charming tale of a caterpillar named Henry as he finds that there is more to life
than simply munching green. He discovers that it is what is inside of us that is most important,
and each of us can learn to fly the skies.

ISBN 0-9704597-7-7
[1. Caterpillar Butterfly-Fiction.   2. Bugs-Children's Fiction.   3. Stories in rhyme]

Printed by
Daehan Printing in South Korea

Illustrations in this book were created on a Macintosh G4 computer using Adobe Photoshop and a mouse!

Visit us for fun and games at:
www.michaelsmind.com

To life! To the heroes and families of New York who remind us its importance; to my friend, Henry Z, who has traveled far in it: to Kathryn, who continues to figure it out; to my family and friends who add so much to it; to Ms. Laflamme's great second grade class so full of it; and to the Father, Son, and Holy Spirit who bring it.

— S.T.

To my country The United States of America.
Land of the free. Home of the brave!

— R.C.

There was a caterpillar
by the name of Henry Hump
his friends were Norm and Stinky
and the lovely Myrtle Munch.

His best friend was Myrtle
with whom he liked to play
she had one eye of blue
her other was light gray.

Norm was a teaser,
we all have met the kind,
he and Stinky laughed
when Henry used his mind.

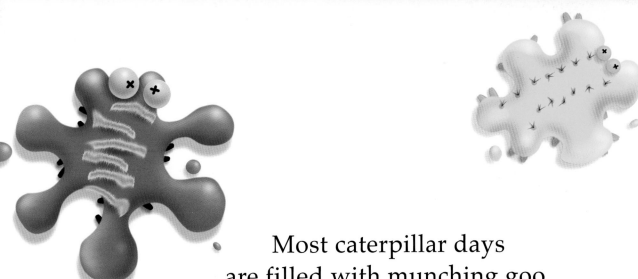

Most caterpillar days
are filled with munching goo,
the sticky stuff inside a leaf
that comes in different hues.

They spend each day crunching
and grinding up a few,
chewing, gnawing, nibbling
then drinking down the brew.

Some goo is red, some yellow
and some is greenish-blue,
if you've ever stepped on one
you know that this is true!

Myrtle with her funny eyes
was with Henry munching brunch,
when Norm and Stinky showed up
to gobble up their leafy lunch.

Whirling as they mowed down
staggering swaths of green,
shearing and slashing,
then slopping up the cream.

Henry stared and said,
"Glittering Gobs of Goo!
Don't you think of anything
but slurping up, you two?"

"Some of us have questions,
don't you even care?
Like who we are, what, or
why we're even here?"

"What is this life we're living?
Who's behind the scene?
There's got to be more here
than slurping green cuisine!"

"Who cares?" called out Stinky,
"come with us and eat!
There's plenty of goo left
in this very tender leaf!"

"No thanks," replied Henry,
"I've been thinking quite a lot,
about why we might be born
on this funny parking lot."

"We are not born here
to eat the biggest bunch,
just feeding endlessly
at some eternal lunch."

"Something's watching over us
and helping us to grow.
We're here to serve a purpose,
what it is I do not know."

"There's more to life than
desserts of which we dream,
more than we can see here,
things hidden and unseen."

"We weren't born here
just to swill this sticky stew,
my mind is telling me
we have other things to do."

"The truth behind our life
that Mystery we can't see
is calling on us all to
be as much as we can be."

Norm looked at Henry,
he thought Henry was a nut.
Stinky, who was bloated,
burped deep inside his gut.
"Sit down, sit down!" they said,
"and slurp up on some goo."

"You'll feel much better fed,
you really know you do.
Eat some of this purple stuff,
it really is divine!
and...PLEASE, won't you
stop thinking all the time?"

Caterpillars spin cocoons,
both you and I know why,
but to a caterpillar
it's a scary do or die.
To our wormy friends
it seems like a knitted tomb

marking the end of life
not just another room.
The little caterpillars
don't know the braided place
will lead them to a new life
where they can fly in space!

Henry was suspicious
he did not like cocoons,
and wasn't very eager
to visit one real soon.

Henry had been noticing
when his buddy bugs went in
another bug came out
and it wasn't his old friend!

Henry was afraid his friends
were menu á la carte
for big bugs with wings
hiding in the woven dark.

Myrtle was the first who
began to dance the weave.
Henry cried that day
not wishing her to leave.

Watching the spinning fog
hanging near the moon,
Henry was convinced
that Myrtle met her doom.

But each must take the nap
or none would learn to fly,
changing slowly in cocoon
until they can glide the sky!

Myrtle spun cocoon
wrapping herself tight
going for a little sleep
in that dark and curious night.

One morning it cracked open,
out fluttered fuzzy wings,
then happened the most amazing
of great and joyous things.

The flying bug saw Henry
and gave a little wink,
taking off for the clouds
with a whistle and a blink.

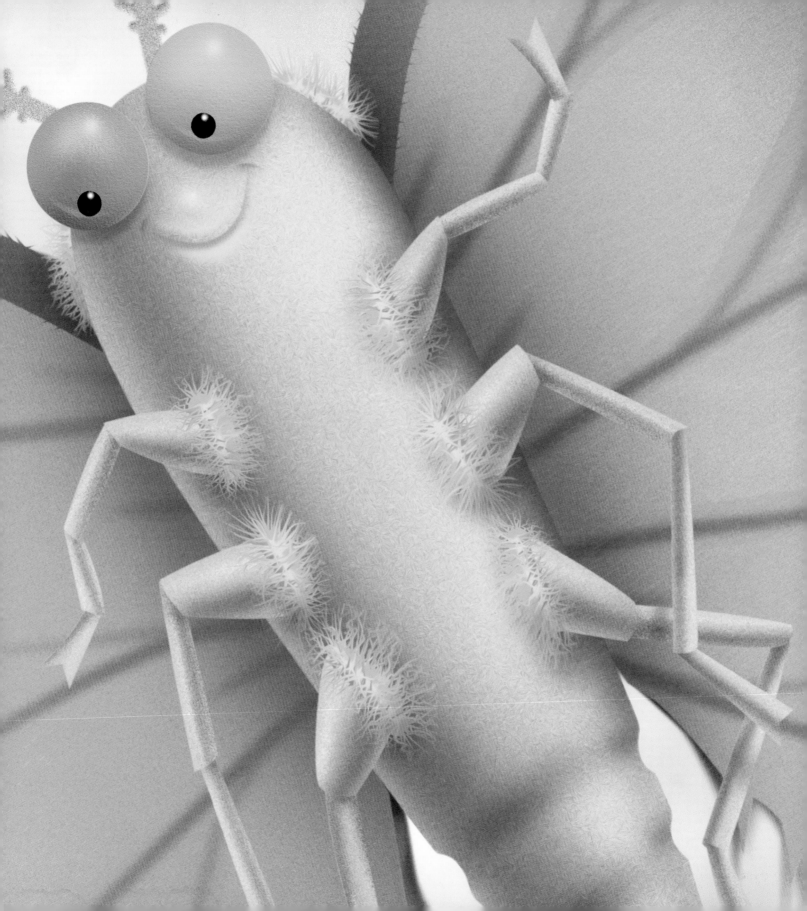

It only took one glance,
a moment to persuade,
Henry's heart leapt with belief
in the dazzling changes made.

For the eyes that winked
at Henry on that day
one eye was dark blue,
the other eye was gray!

Joy welled up in Henry,
wonder swirling in his head
his feet dancing lightly
around Myrtle's vacant bed.

Henry was sure it was
Myrtle on the wing.
His brain began to think
and his heart began to sing.

"There is more here than meets
a young bug's searching eye,
caterpillars were meant
to be up in the sky!"

"Not only greenish glue
will make us all complete.
Inside each of us is more than
the sludgey fudge we eat."

"The truth about our lives
is hidden underneath
sometimes we don't know this
until we look beneath the leaf."

"We all have trust and hope
that helps us to inspire
the people all around us
with dreams and with desire."

"I know we have a purpose,
I see it written in the sky,
the Spirit behind our life
has made us Born to Fly!"

To be continued...

Steve Tiller is described by family and friends as kind, generous, messy, and forgetful. He has the ability to keep himself amused even when nobody else thinks it's all that funny. His girls think he hung the moon- a belief that he does his best to foster. His son thinks...well, you know how sons are. But, the description he likes the best is the one most frequently applied, "He ain't really right, you know!" If you are a child of the South- you won't have to ask what that means.

Husband, Daddy and Computer folk artist **Robert Cremeans** is devoted to his family and his art. He was born and raised in almost heaven West Virginia. Robert graduated from the Columbus College of Art & Design. He now lives in Atlanta with his lovely wife Naomi, his daughter Blue, and his son Noah. An apt description might include "a nice guy, a great artist, a man with a very strange taste in clothes!" He likes to catch crawdads with his kids, and throw snowballs at buses. Luckily it doesn't snow much in Dixie!